Empowering Seniors in the Digital World

C. P. Kumar
Reiki Healer
Roorkee - 247667, India

Disclaimer

While every effort has been made to ensure the accuracy and completeness of the content in this book, the author cannot guarantee that the information contained herein is error-free, up-to-date, or suitable for every individual circumstance.

The author shall not be held liable or responsible for any errors or omissions in the content of the book, nor for any damages, or losses that may arise from any actions taken based upon the suggestions or contents presented in the book.

Readers are advised to use their own judgment and discretion in applying the information provided in this book, and to consult with qualified professionals before taking any action based on the contents of this book. The author disclaims any and all liability or responsibility for any actions taken or not taken based on the information contained in this book.

DEDICATION

To all the seniors who have embarked on the incredible journey of embracing the digital world. Your resilience, curiosity, and determination inspire us all. This book is dedicated to you, the pioneers of a new age, as you navigate the uncharted waters of technology and empower yourselves in ways you never thought possible.

May this guide be your trusted companion on your digital literacy voyage, helping you find the confidence to explore the online realm and connect with your loved ones, learn, and discover the myriad opportunities the digital world has to offer.

You are not alone on this path. Your quest for knowledge, your desire to connect, and your commitment to lifelong learning are truly commendable. Through this dedication, we salute your unwavering spirit and dedication to personal growth.

With heartfelt appreciation for your remarkable journey,

C. P. Kumar

CONTENTS

PREFACE

In today's fast-paced digital age, the world is more connected than ever before, and technology plays an integral role in our daily lives. The digital landscape is continually evolving, and for many, it can feel overwhelming. However, there's a significant segment of our population that may feel left behind in this digital revolution – our seniors.

"Empowering Seniors in the Digital World" is a comprehensive guide crafted with the utmost care and consideration to bridge the digital divide. This book is designed to empower seniors with the knowledge, skills, and confidence they need to navigate the digital realm with ease and grace.

The importance of digital literacy cannot be overstated in today's world. As we delve into this journey, the initial chapters will lay a strong foundation. We start by defining digital literacy, explaining why it's vital for seniors, and shedding light on the far-reaching impact of the digital divide. From this starting point, our journey will evolve to cover a myriad of essential topics, each intended to provide seniors with the tools they need to thrive in the digital age.

"*Getting Started with Technology*" guides you through the process of selecting the right devices and customizing them to suit your preferences. You'll become proficient at navigating various operating systems, from Windows to macOS, Android to iOS, and will feel right at home in the digital world.

Our exploration continues with "*Basic Internet Skills*", where you'll master web browsing, effective use of search engines, and understanding web addresses. Soon, you'll be surfing the internet confidently and efficiently.

Communication is at the heart of the digital experience, and *"Email Communication"* will teach you to create and manage email accounts, send and receive messages, and recognize and avoid email scams. You'll gain valuable insights into keeping your online interactions safe and secure.

As you progress, you'll embark on a journey into the world of *"Social Media and Online Communities"*, setting up profiles on platforms like Facebook and Twitter and learning how to safeguard your privacy online. You'll also develop the skills to protect yourself from online threats through *"Online Safety and Security"*, exploring password management, recognizing and avoiding scams, and securing your personal information.

Digital communication tools are essential for staying connected, and you'll become proficient in *"Digital Communication Tools"*, learning to make video calls, and use messaging apps to connect with loved ones no matter the distance.

"Online Shopping and Banking" covers making secure transactions and shopping safely online. *"Digital Media: Photos and Videos"* empowers you to capture moments, watch and share videos, and use cloud storage services to keep your memories safe.

Your online presence is not only about using technology but also understanding it. In *"Information Literacy"*, you'll discover how to evaluate online information, spot fake news and misinformation, and cite sources appropriately.

Life in the digital age isn't all about work and information; it's about leisure and hobbies too. *"Online Entertainment and Hobbies"* guides you through streaming movies, TV shows, and exploring digital art or online gaming.

When you encounter tech challenges, *"Troubleshooting and Technical Support"* offers practical solutions. Meanwhile, *"Staying Up-to-Date"* ensures you remain current with software and technology trends.

The digital world comes with its own set of rules, which we explore in *"Digital Etiquette and Ethics"*. *"Connecting with Family and Friends"* shows you how to use social media for staying in touch and even hosting online family reunions.

Addressing common fears and building confidence are also key aspects of our journey. *"Building Confidence and Overcoming Fear"* encourages you to tackle your doubts head-on, growing with each new skill you acquire.

We recognize that learning is an ongoing journey. *"Resources for Ongoing Learning"* provides guidance on online courses, local community resources, and offers insights into overcoming challenges and achieving your goals through technology.

Lastly, our *"Glossary of Digital Terms"* serves as a reference point for all the digital terminology you'll encounter throughout this book.

As you embark on this transformative journey, you will not only gain digital skills but also build the confidence and self-assurance to thrive in the digital world. The significance of this endeavor is immeasurable, as it brings empowerment, connection, and new horizons to the lives of seniors.

So, whether you're a senior looking to embrace the digital age or someone assisting a loved one on this journey, "Empowering Seniors in the Digital World" is your trusted guide. Together, let's embrace the boundless opportunities that the digital world has to offer.

C. P. Kumar
Reiki Healer
Former Scientist 'G', National Institute of Hydrology
Roorkee - 247667, India
Web: https://www.angelfire.com/nh/cpkumar/virgo.html

Chapter 1. Introduction to Digital Literacy

In an era where technology is deeply intertwined with our daily lives, the concept of digital literacy has become increasingly vital. As we adapt to the ever-evolving digital landscape, seniors, in particular, are finding themselves at the crossroads of a rapidly changing world. To empower seniors in the digital realm, it is essential to understand and embrace the significance of digital literacy. This article delves into the essence of digital literacy, highlighting its importance for seniors, and addresses the consequences of the digital divide.

Defining Digital Literacy

Digital literacy, at its core, is the ability to use, understand, and navigate digital technology effectively. It encompasses a wide range of skills, from basic to advanced, that allow individuals to interact with digital devices and services. These skills include understanding hardware and software, navigating the internet, managing and evaluating digital information, communicating through various digital platforms, and staying safe in the digital environment.

For seniors, digital literacy means not just being able to use a smartphone or computer but also having the confidence and knowledge to explore the digital world. It includes the ability to perform tasks such as sending emails, conducting online research, using social media, and even managing finances online. Digital literacy for seniors is not about becoming technology experts but about acquiring the necessary skills to lead a more enriched and connected life in the digital age.

Why Digital Literacy is Important for Seniors

Digital literacy is particularly important for seniors for a variety of reasons.

Social Connection: One of the most compelling reasons for seniors to embrace digital literacy is the opportunity it provides for staying connected with loved ones. Digital tools like social media, video calls, and instant messaging apps allow seniors to bridge geographical gaps and maintain relationships with family and friends, even if they are miles away. This is especially significant in today's globalized world, where families often live apart.

Access to Information: The internet is an immense repository of knowledge and information. Digital literacy equips seniors with the ability to access this wealth of information, be it for researching a hobby, staying updated on current events, or simply satisfying their curiosity. This can lead to a more intellectually stimulating and informed life.

Convenience: Digital literacy makes everyday tasks more convenient. Seniors can pay bills, shop for groceries, and access healthcare information and services online. This convenience is particularly beneficial for those who may face mobility or transportation challenges.

Healthcare: With the rise of telemedicine, seniors can now consult with healthcare professionals from the comfort of their homes. Being digitally literate enables them to make appointments, access medical records, and engage in video consultations, promoting better healthcare management.

Mental Stimulation: Engaging with digital technology can be mentally stimulating for seniors. Learning how to use new applications and devices can keep their minds active and foster a sense of accomplishment.

Financial Management: Digital literacy can enhance financial independence for seniors. They can manage their bank accounts online, pay bills electronically, and monitor investments, giving them greater control over their financial affairs.

Emergency Communication: In emergency situations, digital literacy can be a lifesaver. Seniors can use their phones and other digital devices to seek help, send alerts, and stay informed about local emergencies.

Entertainment and Leisure: The digital world offers countless forms of entertainment and leisure activities. Seniors can enjoy online games, watch movies and TV shows, explore virtual museums, and participate in digital art and craft communities.

The Digital Divide and Its Impact

While digital literacy holds significant promise for seniors, a looming challenge stands in the way - the digital divide. The digital divide refers to the gap that exists between those who have access to and knowledge of digital technology and those who do not. This divide is influenced by various factors, including age, income, education, and geographic location. The impact of the digital divide on seniors is substantial.

Social Isolation: Seniors who lack digital literacy skills or access to technology often find themselves socially isolated. As family and friends communicate through digital channels, those left on the other side of the digital divide risk feeling disconnected and lonely.

Limited Access to Services: The digital divide can restrict seniors' access to essential services, such as healthcare, banking, and government services. This limitation can lead to inconvenience, inefficiency, and even exacerbate health issues in the absence of timely access to medical information and services.

Economic Disparities: Seniors on the wrong side of the digital divide may miss out on economic opportunities. Online job searches, freelance work, and remote employment options are becoming increasingly prevalent, but without digital literacy, seniors might be unable to capitalize on these opportunities.

Healthcare Disparities: The digital divide can exacerbate healthcare disparities among seniors. Those who are digitally literate can take advantage of telehealth services and stay on top of their health, while those without digital skills may face obstacles in accessing essential healthcare information and services.

Safety Concerns: Seniors who lack digital literacy can be more vulnerable to online scams and cyberattacks. Without the knowledge to protect themselves online, they may inadvertently expose themselves to financial and personal risks.

Dependence on Others: When seniors do not have digital literacy skills, they often depend on others, such as family members, for essential tasks like online banking, appointment scheduling, and shopping. This can be disempowering and may lead to a loss of independence.

Conclusion

Digital literacy is not just a skill; it is a gateway to an empowered and fulfilling life in the modern world. For seniors, in particular, digital literacy opens doors to social connection, information, convenience, and much more. It is a bridge across the digital divide, allowing seniors to navigate the digital landscape with confidence and purpose.

However, the digital divide remains a significant obstacle. It is essential for society, governments, and community organizations to take proactive steps in bridging this divide. By providing digital literacy training, ensuring affordable access to technology, and promoting digital inclusion, we can empower seniors to lead healthier, more connected, and independent lives in the digital age.

Empowering seniors in the digital world is not just a matter of imparting skills but also of enriching lives and fostering a sense of belonging in an increasingly digital society. By recognizing the importance of digital literacy for seniors and addressing the digital divide, we can ensure that they are not left behind but rather actively engaged in the exciting possibilities of the digital era.

Chapter 2. Getting Started with Technology

Introduction

In an age dominated by technology, digital literacy has become essential for people of all generations, including seniors. The world's technological landscape is constantly evolving, making it necessary for seniors to embark on their digital journeys. Embracing technology can enrich the lives of seniors, offering new opportunities for connection, information, and convenience. This article explores the key steps seniors should consider when entering the digital realm, from choosing the right devices to setting them up and customizing the user experience.

Choosing the Right Devices

Selecting the appropriate devices is the first step in the journey towards becoming tech-savvy. Seniors have a range of choices, each suited to different needs and preferences.

Computers: Personal computers, such as desktops and laptops, offer versatility and larger screens. They are ideal for tasks that require a keyboard, like word processing, browsing the web, and using various software applications.

Smartphones: Smartphones are pocket-sized powerhouses, providing easy access to calls, messaging, emails, web browsing, and countless apps. They are particularly convenient for on-the-go communication and information.

Tablets: Tablets offer a compromise between the mobility of smartphones and the screen size of computers. They are great for reading e-books, watching videos, browsing the web, and playing games. Tablets are often more user-friendly due to their touch interfaces.

E-Readers: For book lovers, e-readers like Kindle are a great choice. They are designed for reading e-books and offer an exceptional reading experience with features like adjustable font size and screen glare reduction.

When choosing a device, consider factors like screen size, weight, battery life, ease of use, and your specific needs. It's important to remember that devices come in various operating systems, such as Windows, macOS, Android, and iOS. The choice of operating system can significantly impact the user experience, so it's worth researching and considering which one aligns with your preferences.

Setting Up and Customizing Devices

Once you've selected your device, it's time to set it up and customize it to suit your needs. Here are the steps to get started:

Unboxing and Assembly: Carefully unbox your device and follow the provided instructions for assembly. Be sure to keep any accompanying manuals for reference.

Charging: Most devices come with some initial charge, but it's a good idea to fully charge your device before use. This ensures you won't run out of power during the setup process.

Turning It On: Power up your device by pressing the power button or, in the case of smartphones and tablets, holding down the power button until the screen lights up.

Initial Setup: Follow the on-screen prompts to complete the initial setup. This typically includes selecting your language, connecting to Wi-Fi, and signing in with or creating an account, depending on the device.

Updates: After the initial setup, your device may prompt you to install updates. These updates are essential for security and performance, so it's advisable to let them install.

Personalization: Customize your device by adjusting settings like screen brightness, text size, and sound preferences. You can also personalize the device's background or home screen with your favorite images.

Installing Apps: Depending on your device, you may want to install various applications, like email, messaging, web browsers, and games. Visit your device's app store or marketplace to browse and download apps.

Navigating the Operating System

Navigating the operating system is a fundamental aspect of using digital devices effectively. The interface and navigation methods vary between operating systems, so let's explore some key points for the most common ones.

Windows: If you're using a Windows PC or laptop, you'll find yourself navigating the desktop. The Start menu, usually located in the lower-left corner of the screen, is your gateway to applications, settings, and files. You can pin your most-used apps to the taskbar for quick access. To explore further, the File Explorer is where you can manage your files and folders.

macOS: On Mac computers, the Dock at the bottom of the screen serves as a quick-launch bar for your favorite applications. The Apple menu (Apple icon in the upper-left corner) provides access to settings and system preferences. The Finder is macOS's counterpart to Windows' File Explorer, used for file management.

Android: Android is the operating system used on a wide range of smartphones and tablets. Navigating the Android interface involves swiping up from the bottom to access the app drawer, swiping down from the top to reveal notifications and quick settings, and using the home button or gestures to switch between apps.

iOS: iOS powers Apple's iPhone and iPad. The home screen is filled with app icons. Swipe down from the top to access notifications and control center. Use gestures like swiping from the bottom to go back to the home screen or switching between apps.

It's crucial to familiarize yourself with the basic navigation principles of your chosen operating system. Most devices offer user guides and tutorials to help you get started. Additionally, you can find a wealth of online tutorials and videos that provide step-by-step instructions for using your specific device and operating system.

Conclusion

For seniors, getting started with technology is an exciting journey that can bring new opportunities, connectivity, and convenience to their lives. Choosing the right device, setting it up, and customizing it to personal preferences are essential initial steps. As you become more comfortable with your device, learning to navigate the operating system is the key to unlocking its full potential.

Remember that technology is meant to serve your needs and enhance your daily life. It's normal to face challenges along the way, but don't be discouraged. With patience, practice, and access to resources like user manuals and online tutorials, you can become proficient in using your chosen digital device. By taking the initiative to embrace technology, seniors can embark on a fulfilling digital journey that leads to a more enriched, connected, and empowered life in the digital world.

Introduction

In the ever-expanding digital landscape, the internet has become a vital tool for staying connected, accessing information, and participating in the modern world. For seniors looking to empower themselves in the digital age, acquiring basic internet skills is a crucial step. In this article, we will explore the essential skills that seniors need to navigate the internet effectively. From browsing the web to understanding web addresses and using search engines, these skills will open up a world of knowledge and connectivity.

Browsing the Web

Browsing the web is the gateway to a vast reservoir of information, services, and entertainment. Here are some key aspects to consider when navigating the online world:

Web Browsers: A web browser is a software application that allows you to access and explore the internet. Some popular web browsers include Google Chrome, Mozilla Firefox, Microsoft Edge, and Apple Safari. Choose one that suits your needs and install it on your device.

Opening a Web Browser: To start browsing the web, open your chosen web browser. You can typically find the browser icon on your device's desktop or applications folder. Click or tap on it to launch the browser.

Using the Address Bar: The address bar, often located at the top of the browser window, is where you type the web address, known as a URL, to visit a specific website. To access a website, simply click on the address bar, type the URL (e.g., www.google.com), and press Enter on your keyboard or tap "Go" on a touchscreen device.

Tabs: Web browsers allow you to open multiple web pages in separate tabs. This makes it easy to switch between different websites. To open a new tab, click the "+" button next to an open tab or use keyboard shortcuts (e.g., Ctrl + T on Windows, Command + T on macOS).

Navigating Websites: Once you've opened a website, you can navigate it by clicking on links and buttons, scrolling down the page, and using the back and forward buttons to move between pages.

Bookmarks: To save websites you frequently visit, you can create bookmarks. This way, you can easily access your favorite websites with a single click. Most browsers have a "Bookmark" or "Favorites" menu for managing your saved sites.

Using Search Engines Effectively

Search engines are powerful tools that help you find information on the internet. They are particularly useful for locating websites, articles, videos, and other digital content. Google is one of the most popular search engines, but there are many others like Bing and Yahoo. Here's how to use search engines effectively:

Accessing a Search Engine: To use a search engine, open your web browser and type the search engine's URL in the address bar (e.g., www.google.com) or simply use the browser's default search bar, which is typically located at the top of the browser window.

Entering a Search Query: In the search bar, type a question, phrase, or keywords related to the information you're looking for. For example, if you want to learn about gardening tips, you could type "gardening tips for beginners."

Reviewing Search Results: After pressing Enter, the search engine will display a list of search results. These results are typically ranked by relevance, with the most relevant results appearing at the top. Click on a search result to visit the website or article.

Refining Your Search: If your initial search doesn't yield the desired results, you can refine it by adding more specific keywords or using quotation marks to search for exact phrases. For example, you can search for "organic gardening tips".

Using Filters: Some search engines offer filters to narrow down search results. You can filter results by time, type (e.g., images, videos), and location.

Understanding Web Addresses (URLs)

A URL, or Uniform Resource Locator, is the web address of a specific webpage or website. Understanding URLs is crucial for navigating the web and visiting websites directly. A URL typically consists of the following components:

Protocol: The protocol defines how the web browser should retrieve the webpage. The most common protocol is "http" (Hypertext Transfer Protocol) or "https" (Hypertext Transfer Protocol Secure). The latter is more secure and is commonly used for websites that require user input or personal information.

Domain Name: The domain name is the human-readable address of a website. For example, in the URL "https://www.example.com," "www.example.com" is the domain name.

Top-Level Domain (TLD): The TLD is the suffix that indicates the type or purpose of the website. Common TLDs include ".com," ".org," ".net," and country-specific TLDs like ".uk" for the United Kingdom.

Path: The path specifies the specific webpage or directory within the website. For example, in "https://www.example.com/blog," "/blog" is the path.

Query String: In some URLs, you may see a query string, which is a set of parameters that the website uses to fetch specific content. It's often preceded by a question mark, like in "https://www.example.com/search?q=senior+tech".

Understanding these components can help you interpret and enter web addresses correctly. It's important to be cautious when entering sensitive information on websites, especially if they do not have the "https" protocol, as it indicates a secure connection.

Conclusion

Basic internet skills are essential for seniors to unlock the vast potential of the digital world. Browsing the web, using search engines effectively, and understanding web addresses are fundamental abilities that open doors to information, communication, and entertainment.

As seniors embrace these skills, they gain access to a wealth of knowledge and connectivity, which can enrich their lives in numerous ways. By developing these skills and becoming confident internet users, seniors can explore the digital world with ease and reap the benefits it has to offer, from staying informed to connecting with loved ones and accessing a world of resources and entertainment.

Chapter 4. Email Communication

Introduction

In the age of instant messaging and social media, email remains a powerful and essential means of digital communication. For seniors looking to empower themselves in the digital world, mastering email communication is a valuable skill. This article delves into the world of email, from creating and managing email accounts to sending and receiving messages. It also addresses the critical aspect of recognizing and avoiding email scams, ensuring that seniors can navigate the world of electronic communication safely and effectively.

Creating and Managing Email Accounts

Email communication begins with creating an email account and managing it effectively. Here's how to get started:

1. Choosing an Email Service: There are various email service providers available, such as Gmail, Yahoo Mail, Outlook (formerly Hotmail), and Apple Mail. You can choose the one that suits your preferences. Many of these services offer free email accounts, and some may require you to create an account using a mobile phone number.

2. Signing Up: To create an email account, visit the website of your chosen email service provider and look for a sign-up or create an account option. You'll be asked to provide some personal information, including your name, desired email address, and a password.

3. Selecting an Email Address: Your email address is your online identity. It should be unique and easily memorable for you. Many times, your chosen email service provider may suggest variations of your preferred email address if your first choice is already taken.

4. Creating a Strong Password: It's important to create a strong, unique password to protect your email account. A strong password typically includes a combination of uppercase and lowercase letters, numbers, and special characters. Avoid using easily guessable information like birthdays or names.

5. Verification: After filling out the required information, you'll usually receive a verification email or code to confirm your account. Follow the provided instructions to verify your email address.

6. Managing Your Email Account: Once your email account is created, you can access it by visiting the email service provider's website and logging in using your email address and password. Most email services offer user-friendly interfaces for managing your account, including settings, security options, and contact management.

Sending and Receiving Emails

After creating your email account, it's time to start sending and receiving emails. Here's how to do it effectively:

1. Composing an Email: To compose a new email, log in to your email account and look for a "Compose" or "New" button. Clicking this button will open a window where you can enter the recipient's email address, subject, and the body of the email.

2. Adding Attachments: You can include attachments in your emails, such as documents, images, or files. Look for an attachment icon or option in the email composition window to attach files from your computer or device.

3. Formatting Your Email: Most email services provide formatting options, allowing you to change the font, style, and add formatting to your email text. You can also include links and images within your messages.

4. Sending Your Email: After composing your email, click the "Send" button to send it. The email will be delivered to the recipient's email address, and they will receive a notification of the new message.

5. Checking Your Inbox: To check your incoming emails, simply log in to your email account and navigate to your inbox. New messages will appear here, and you can click on them to read the content.

6. Replying to Emails: When you receive an email, you can reply by opening the email and clicking the "Reply" or "Reply All" button. "Reply" sends your response only to the sender, while "Reply All" sends it to all recipients.

7. Forwarding Emails: You can also forward emails to others by clicking the "Forward" option and entering the email addresses of the recipients.

Recognizing and Avoiding Email Scams

Email scams are a significant concern in the digital world. Seniors, in particular, need to be cautious when opening emails to avoid falling victim to scams. Here are some common email scams to be aware of and how to avoid them:

1. Phishing Emails: Phishing emails attempt to trick you into revealing personal or financial information by pretending to be from a trusted source, such as a bank, government agency, or a popular service like PayPal. Be cautious when opening emails from unknown sources and avoid clicking on suspicious links or providing personal information.

2. Spam Emails: Spam emails are unsolicited messages that can clutter your inbox. Most email services have spam filters that automatically detect and move spam emails to a designated folder. Be cautious about opening emails from unknown senders.

3. Chain Emails: Chain emails often contain exaggerated or false stories and encourage you to forward the email to others. These emails are typically harmless but can be annoying. Avoid forwarding chain emails and consider marking them as spam.

4. Fake Prize or Lottery Emails: Emails claiming that you've won a prize or a lottery are usually scams. Be skeptical of emails promising unexpected winnings and never provide personal or financial information in response to such emails.

5. Malware or Virus Emails: Some emails contain attachments or links that can infect your computer or device with malware or viruses. Avoid opening attachments or clicking on links in emails from unknown or suspicious sources.

6. Charity Scams: Be cautious about emails requesting donations or funds for charitable causes. If you want to

support a charity, visit their official website to make a donation rather than responding to email requests.

7. Recognizing Legitimate Emails: Legitimate organizations, such as your bank or government agencies, will not ask for sensitive information via email. Be skeptical of any email requesting personal, financial, or login information and verify the source by contacting the organization directly using official contact information.

Conclusion

Email communication is a valuable skill that opens doors to connectivity, information sharing, and online correspondence. By creating and managing email accounts, sending and receiving emails, and being aware of email scams, seniors can make the most of this digital tool safely and effectively.

As seniors empower themselves in the digital world, mastering email communication allows them to stay in touch with loved ones, access valuable information, and communicate with organizations and services. With the right knowledge and cautious online behavior, seniors can harness the power of email to enrich their lives and enhance their digital experience.

Chapter 5. Social Media and Online Communities

Introduction

The digital world is a vast landscape, and one of its most dynamic aspects is social media. As seniors embrace the digital age, understanding social media and online communities is essential for staying connected, informed, and engaged. In this article, we'll explore the realm of social media platforms, how to set up profiles, and crucial tips for maintaining safety and privacy. By empowering seniors with the knowledge to navigate these digital spaces, they can experience the benefits and joys of online communities.

Introduction to Social Media Platforms

Social media platforms are online spaces where individuals can connect with friends, family, and people from around the world. They enable sharing thoughts, photos, videos, and updates, making it easier to stay in touch and engage with others. Let's explore some popular social media platforms:

1. Facebook: Facebook is one of the most well-known social media platforms. Users create profiles, connect with friends, and share text, photos, and videos. It's a platform for staying connected with loved ones and joining groups or communities based on shared interests.

2. Twitter: Twitter is a microblogging platform where users post short messages, or tweets, to their followers. It's

known for its real-time updates, news sharing, and following celebrities and organizations.

3. Instagram: Instagram is a visual platform centered on sharing photos and short videos. Users can follow friends and influencers and explore a variety of images and content.

4. LinkedIn: LinkedIn is a professional networking platform that focuses on career-related connections. Users can create a profile that highlights their skills and experience, connect with colleagues, and explore job opportunities.

5. Pinterest: Pinterest is a platform for discovering and saving ideas, primarily through images and links. Users can create boards to organize content related to hobbies, recipes, home decor, and more.

6. YouTube: While not a traditional social media platform, YouTube is a place for sharing and watching videos. Users can subscribe to channels, comment on videos, and create their own content.

Setting Up Social Media Profiles

Creating and setting up profiles on social media platforms is relatively straightforward, but it's essential to do so mindfully. Here's a general guide for setting up a social media profile:

1. Choose a Platform: Decide which social media platform you'd like to join based on your interests and the type of connections you wish to make.

2. Create an Account: Visit the platform's website or app, and look for a "Sign Up" or "Create Account" option. You'll typically need to provide a valid email address and create a password.

3. Complete Your Profile: Most platforms will guide you through the process of completing your profile. You'll be asked for your name, a profile picture (usually a photo of yourself), and some basic information.

4. Adjust Privacy Settings: Review and adjust your privacy settings to control who can see your posts and connect with you. These settings are usually found in the platform's account or settings section.

5. Add Friends or Connections: To get started, you can search for friends or people you know and send them friend or connection requests. You can also join groups or communities related to your interests.

6. Share Content: Start sharing content, such as text posts, photos, or videos. You can share updates about your life, your hobbies, or share interesting articles or posts you find online.

Staying Safe and Private on Social Media

While social media can be a wonderful way to connect with others, it's essential to stay safe and protect your privacy online. Here are some crucial tips for staying safe on social media:

1. Be Cautious with Personal Information: Avoid sharing sensitive personal information, such as your home address, phone number, or financial details, on social media. Be mindful of the information you provide in your profile.

2. Adjust Privacy Settings: **Review and customize your privacy settings to control who can see your content and connect with you. On platforms like Facebook, you can create custom friend lists to share specific posts with selected friends.**

3. Verify Requests: **When you receive friend or connection requests, verify the identity of the person sending the request. Be cautious about accepting requests from unknown or suspicious accounts.**

4. Be Wary of Scams: **Social media can be a breeding ground for scams. Be cautious of unsolicited messages or friend requests from unknown individuals, and avoid clicking on links or downloading files from unverified sources.**

5. Think Before You Post: **Before posting anything, consider the potential consequences. Remember that once you post something online, it can be challenging to remove entirely. Be mindful of your language, tone, and the impact your posts may have on others.**

6. Use Strong Passwords: **Ensure that you use strong, unique passwords for your social media accounts. It's a good practice to change your password regularly and enable two-factor authentication when available.**

7. Beware of Phishing: **Be cautious of emails or messages that claim to be from a social media platform and ask for your login credentials. Always verify the legitimacy of such requests before responding.**

8. Educate Yourself: **Stay informed about common online scams and threats, and be vigilant about online safety.**

Many resources are available online to help you recognize and avoid potential risks.

9. Report and Block: Most social media platforms offer options to report and block users who engage in abusive or inappropriate behavior. Don't hesitate to use these features if needed.

Conclusion

Social media and online communities can be a source of great joy, connection, and information for seniors in the digital world. By exploring platforms like Facebook, Twitter, Instagram, and more, seniors can stay connected with friends and family, discover new interests, and engage with communities that share their passions.

To make the most of these platforms, it's important to create profiles thoughtfully, maintain privacy, and be vigilant about online safety. By following best practices, seniors can enjoy the benefits of social media while staying secure in the digital landscape. Embracing social media can be a transformative experience, enriching the lives of seniors by expanding their digital horizons and empowering them to connect with the world in new and exciting ways.

Chapter 6. Online Safety and Security

Introduction

In today's rapidly evolving digital landscape, online safety and security are critical concerns for people of all ages, but they hold particular importance for seniors who are relatively new to the digital world. As more aspects of our lives shift online, it's essential for seniors to navigate the digital realm with confidence and security. This article explores the various aspects of online safety and security, with a focus on empowering seniors to protect themselves in the vast online wilderness.

Password Management

1. The Importance of Strong Passwords

One of the fundamental pillars of online safety is password management. Seniors should understand the importance of creating strong and unique passwords for their various online accounts. A strong password typically includes a combination of uppercase and lowercase letters, numbers, and special characters. It should be unrelated to easily accessible personal information like birthdays, names, or common words.

2. Password Managers

For seniors who may find it challenging to remember numerous complex passwords, password managers can be a valuable tool. These applications generate and securely store passwords for different websites, allowing seniors to access their accounts with a single master password.

Popular password managers include LastPass, 1Password, and Dashlane.

3. Password Hygiene

Regularly changing passwords and avoiding the use of the same password across multiple accounts is essential. It's advisable to change passwords every few months and enable two-factor authentication (2FA) whenever possible. 2FA adds an extra layer of security by requiring users to provide a second piece of information, such as a code sent to their mobile device, in addition to their password.

Recognizing and Avoiding Online Scams

1. Common Types of Online Scams

Seniors must be aware of the various online scams that exist, as scammers often target older individuals. Some common types of scams include phishing emails, which masquerade as legitimate messages but are designed to steal personal information, and fake tech support calls claiming to fix non-existent computer issues for a fee. There are also lottery and prize scams, romance scams, and investment scams.

2. Red Flags to Watch For

Seniors should be vigilant and look out for red flags that might indicate a scam. These red flags can include unsolicited requests for personal or financial information, offers that sound too good to be true, or urgent demands for immediate action. Remind seniors to verify the legitimacy of any request before providing sensitive information or making payments.

3. How to Protect Against Scams

Educating seniors about scam prevention is vital. Encourage them to double-check the legitimacy of any unsolicited communication, whether it's an email, phone call, or message on social media. They should never provide personal or financial information to unknown or unverified sources. By following these precautions, seniors can significantly reduce their risk of falling victim to online scams.

Protecting Personal Information Online

1. Understanding the Value of Personal Information

Seniors must realize that their personal information is incredibly valuable to malicious actors. This information includes their name, address, date of birth, social security number, and financial data. Protecting this information is essential for maintaining online safety.

2. Secure Browsing and Safe Websites

When browsing the internet, seniors should prioritize secure websites that encrypt their data. This is indicated by a padlock icon in the browser's address bar and a URL that starts with "https". Encourage seniors to use secure, reputable websites for online shopping and financial transactions, and to be cautious about sharing personal information on unfamiliar websites.

3. Privacy Settings on Social Media

If seniors use social media platforms, they should be aware of the privacy settings available. These settings allow them to control who can see their posts and personal information.

Encourage seniors to review and adjust these settings to limit their exposure to strangers or unwanted individuals.

4. Safe Online Shopping and Banking

Online shopping and banking can be convenient for seniors, but it's crucial to emphasize the importance of secure transactions. Seniors should use strong, unique passwords for their online banking and shopping accounts, and they should regularly monitor their accounts for any suspicious activity. Additionally, they should avoid making financial transactions or sharing personal information over public Wi-Fi networks, as these networks are more susceptible to interception.

5. Email and Social Media Safety

Email is a common avenue for phishing scams, so seniors should be cautious when opening attachments or clicking on links in unsolicited emails. Additionally, they should avoid oversharing on social media. Remind seniors that posting sensitive information like their address, phone number, or travel plans on public platforms can put them at risk.

6. Updates and Security Software

Seniors should ensure that their devices, including computers, smartphones, and tablets, are regularly updated with the latest security patches and software updates. Outdated software can have security vulnerabilities that cybercriminals exploit.

7. Regular Backups

Encourage seniors to regularly back up their important files and data. This can help protect against data loss due to cyberattacks or technical issues. Regular backups should be stored in a secure location, such as an external hard drive or a cloud-based service.

Conclusion

As the digital world becomes an integral part of daily life, online safety and security are paramount for seniors and individuals of all age groups. By understanding the significance of strong password management, recognizing and avoiding online scams, and protecting personal information, seniors can confidently navigate the digital landscape while safeguarding their privacy and security.

Empowering seniors in the digital world requires ongoing education and awareness. It is essential for seniors to stay informed about the latest online threats and to continually update their knowledge and practices. By following the guidelines outlined in this article, seniors can enjoy the many benefits of the digital world while minimizing the risks associated with online activities.

In a rapidly evolving digital landscape, knowledge is power, and seniors have the capability to stay safe and secure online, enabling them to fully embrace the opportunities and conveniences of the digital age.

Chapter 7. Digital Communication Tools

Introduction

In today's fast-paced digital age, communication has evolved, becoming more accessible and dynamic. For seniors, embracing digital communication tools can open up new avenues for connecting with loved ones, engaging in social activities, and staying informed. This article explores the various aspects of digital communication tools, focusing on how seniors can harness these technologies to enhance their connectivity and communication in the modern world.

Making Video Calls: Bridging the Distance

1. The Power of Video Calls

Video calls have revolutionized the way people connect, providing an immersive and personal way to communicate with friends and family, regardless of geographical barriers. For seniors, video calls can be a powerful tool for maintaining meaningful connections with loved ones who may be far away.

2. Popular Video Call Platforms

Skype: Skype is one of the pioneering platforms for video calls, offering both video and voice calling features. It's user-friendly and compatible with various devices, making it an excellent choice for seniors.

Zoom: Zoom is a versatile platform known for its high-quality video and audio. It's widely used for video conferences, making it suitable for seniors who want to participate in group chats or meetings.

3. Getting Started with Video Calls

For seniors who are new to video calling, getting started is easier than one might think. They need to install the chosen app on their device, create an account, and then follow a few simple steps to make their first call. Demonstrating the process and providing step-by-step guidance can help seniors gain confidence in using video call platforms.

4. Staying Connected with Family and Friends

The ability to see loved ones' faces during a conversation can make video calls a particularly powerful tool for seniors. Encourage them to schedule regular video calls with family and friends, which can help combat feelings of isolation and strengthen emotional bonds.

Using Messaging Apps: Quick and Convenient Communication

1. Messaging Apps: A Versatile Choice

Messaging apps offer seniors a quick and convenient way to stay in touch with others. These apps are ideal for text-based communication, sharing photos, and even making voice and video calls.

2. Popular Messaging Apps

WhatsApp: WhatsApp is a widely used messaging app known for its ease of use. It allows users to send text messages, make voice and video calls, and share multimedia content with their contacts.

Facebook Messenger: Seniors who are already familiar with Facebook can use Messenger to chat with friends and family. It provides text, voice, and video messaging options.

3. Getting Started with Messaging Apps

Setting up and using messaging apps is typically straightforward. Users need to download the app, create an account, and then add their contacts. Seniors can explore the various features, including sending text messages, photos, and even making voice or video calls.

4. Engaging in Group Chats

Messaging apps enable seniors to engage in group chats, where they can connect with multiple friends or family members simultaneously. These group chats can be a valuable tool for coordinating events, sharing updates, and staying connected with various circles of friends and loved ones.

5. Sharing Photos and Videos

Messaging apps make it easy for seniors to share photos and videos, allowing them to visually connect with others and share cherished memories. This feature can be especially meaningful for seniors who want to share family photos or moments from special occasions.

Conclusion

Digital communication tools have transformed the way we connect and interact with others. For seniors, embracing these tools can be a gateway to a more connected and vibrant life. Whether through video calls or messaging apps, seniors can leverage technology to maintain close relationships, foster social connections, and stay informed.

By using platforms like Skype and Zoom, seniors can bridge geographical distances and enjoy the benefits of face-to-face communication with loved ones. The process of getting started is relatively simple, and with a little guidance, seniors can become proficient at using these tools to stay connected with family and friends.

Messaging apps like WhatsApp and Facebook Messenger offer convenience and versatility in communication. Seniors can use these apps for text-based messaging, voice and video calls, sharing multimedia content, and engaging in group chats. This flexibility empowers seniors to communicate with multiple contacts, share memories through photos and videos, and keep in touch with friends and family, even if they are miles apart.

In the digital age, connectivity is at our fingertips, and seniors have the opportunity to embrace these tools to enhance their quality of life. By empowering seniors with the knowledge and skills to use digital communication tools effectively, we can bridge generational and geographical gaps, making the world a smaller and more connected place for everyone.

Chapter 8. Online Shopping and Banking

Introduction

The digital age has ushered in an era of convenience and accessibility in various aspects of our lives, and one of the most notable areas where this transformation is evident is online shopping and banking. For seniors who may be new to the digital world, these activities can be both empowering and daunting. This article delves into the intricacies of online shopping and banking, equipping seniors with the knowledge and confidence to navigate the digital landscape securely.

Making Secure Online Transactions

1. The Digital Economy: Embracing Change

The growth of e-commerce has paved the way for a world of possibilities for seniors. Online shopping and banking can save time and energy, offering a variety of products and services at one's fingertips. To partake in this digital economy safely, seniors must understand how to make secure online transactions.

2. Importance of Cybersecurity

The foundation of secure online transactions lies in cybersecurity. Seniors should be aware of common threats such as phishing scams, malware, and identity theft. Understanding these threats is crucial for avoiding them.

3. Choosing Trusted Websites

Before making any online purchase, it's essential to ensure the website is legitimate and secure. Look for secure website indicators like "https://" in the URL and a padlock symbol in the address bar. Seniors should only shop on trusted websites and avoid making purchases from unknown or suspicious sources.

4. Payment Methods

Explaining the various payment methods available is crucial. Seniors can use credit cards, debit cards, digital wallets like PayPal, and even prepaid cards. Each payment method has its pros and cons, and it's vital to discuss these with seniors to help them make informed choices.

5. Using Secure Networks

Seniors should only make online transactions using secure and trusted networks. Public Wi-Fi networks are not as secure, making it important to avoid conducting financial activities, such as online banking, while connected to public Wi-Fi.

Shopping Safely Online

1. Safe Shopping Practices

Online shopping can be an enjoyable experience, provided seniors follow safe shopping practices. This includes being cautious when sharing personal information, and avoiding oversharing on social media platforms. It's essential to educate seniors about the risks of posting information like travel plans or their location, which can be exploited by cybercriminals.

2. Reading Reviews and Product Descriptions

Encourage seniors to read product reviews and descriptions before making a purchase. This can help them understand the quality and credibility of the product or service they're considering. They should also consider the reputation of the seller or website.

3. Returns and Refunds

Seniors should be aware of the return and refund policies of the online store they are buying from. In case they receive a damaged or unsatisfactory product, they should know how to initiate a return or request a refund.

4. Online Shopping Tools

Online shopping tools, such as price comparison websites and browser extensions, can help seniors find the best deals and discounts. Demonstrating how to use these tools can enhance the online shopping experience and ensure they make cost-effective choices.

Online Banking Basics

1. The Convenience of Online Banking

Online banking allows seniors to manage their finances from the comfort of their homes. They can check account balances, pay bills, transfer money, and even set up automatic payments. These capabilities can significantly simplify financial management.

2. Setting Up Online Banking

To get started with online banking, seniors should contact their bank to set up online access. Typically, this involves creating a username and a secure password. It's crucial to choose a strong password that includes a combination of letters, numbers, and special characters.

3. Two-Factor Authentication (2FA)

Encourage seniors to enable two-factor authentication (2FA) for their online banking accounts. This extra layer of security requires them to provide a secondary piece of information, such as a code sent to their mobile device, in addition to their password.

4. Navigating the Online Banking Portal

Familiarizing seniors with the online banking portal is essential. They should know how to check their account balance, view transactions, pay bills, transfer funds, and set up recurring payments. It's also essential to emphasize the importance of logging out of their online banking session and closing the browser when they are done.

5. Avoiding Phishing Scams

Seniors should be cautious about emails or messages that ask for personal or financial information. Remind them that their bank will never request such information through email. If they receive a suspicious email, they should contact their bank directly to verify its authenticity.

Conclusion

Online shopping and banking have become integral parts of our lives, offering seniors unprecedented convenience and accessibility. However, with this convenience comes the responsibility of ensuring the safety and security of one's financial transactions and personal information.

By understanding the importance of cybersecurity, choosing trusted websites, and using secure networks, seniors can make secure online transactions. Safe shopping practices, including reading reviews, understanding return policies, and using online shopping tools, can enhance the online shopping experience and help seniors make informed decisions.

Online banking, when approached with a security-first mindset, can simplify financial management. Seniors can set up online banking, enable two-factor authentication (2FA), and navigate the online banking portal with confidence. It is crucial to stay vigilant against phishing scams and prioritize the security of their financial information.

Empowering seniors in the digital world means equipping them with the knowledge and skills to navigate online shopping and banking safely and confidently. With the right guidance and awareness, seniors can embrace the digital landscape, improving their quality of life and taking full advantage of the conveniences it offers.

Chapter 9. Digital Media: Photos and Videos

Introduction

The digital revolution has transformed how we capture, store, and share visual memories. For seniors, embracing digital media, including photos and videos, can provide a powerful means of preserving and sharing cherished moments. This article explores the various aspects of digital media, offering seniors insights into taking and storing photos, watching and sharing videos, and using cloud storage services to navigate the digital landscape confidently.

Taking and Storing Photos

1. The Power of Digital Photography

The rise of digital photography has made it easier than ever to capture and store images. Seniors can now create lasting memories with their smartphones, digital cameras, or tablets. Encouraging seniors to explore the world of digital photography can be a wonderful way to preserve moments and experiences.

2. Basic Camera Operations

Seniors may need assistance with basic camera operations. This includes understanding how to turn the camera on and off, adjusting the zoom, and switching between photo and video modes. Teaching seniors to take photos and videos is an excellent way to enhance their digital literacy.

3. Storage Options

Discussing storage options for digital photos and videos is crucial. Seniors can store their media on various devices, such as their smartphones, tablets, or computers. Remind them to regularly back up their content to avoid potential loss due to device malfunction or accidental deletion.

4. Organizing Photos and Videos

Teaching seniors how to organize their digital media is vital. They can create folders or albums to categorize their photos and videos, making it easier to find specific memories. Consider demonstrating how to use features like tags, captions, and geotagging to enhance organization.

Watching and Sharing Videos

1. Enjoying Digital Videos

Seniors can enjoy digital videos in various ways, from watching family movies to streaming content online. For many, the advent of digital videos has expanded the world of entertainment and learning.

2. Streaming Services

Seniors can access a plethora of content through streaming services like Netflix, Amazon Prime, Hulu, and YouTube. These services offer a wide range of movies, TV shows, and educational videos. Explaining how to browse and select content on these platforms can enhance their viewing experience.

3. Sharing Videos with Loved Ones

Digital videos are a wonderful way to share experiences with family and friends, especially when distance separates loved ones. Seniors can learn to share videos via email, social media, or cloud storage services. Emphasize the importance of privacy settings when sharing videos online.

4. Editing and Enhancing Videos

Seniors may be interested in editing their videos to create compilations or add special effects. Introducing them to basic video editing software or mobile apps can open up creative possibilities. It's important to start with user-friendly tools and provide step-by-step guidance.

Using Cloud Storage Services

1. The Advantages of Cloud Storage

Cloud storage services offer a secure and convenient way to store, access, and share digital media. Seniors can benefit from using these services to safeguard their photos and videos while making them easily accessible from various devices.

2. Popular Cloud Storage Services

Google Drive: Google Drive provides a seamless experience for those who use Google products. It offers a significant amount of free storage and integrates with Google Photos for easy photo and video backup.

Apple iCloud: Seniors with Apple devices can take advantage of iCloud for storage. iCloud offers synchronization across Apple devices and automatic backup of photos and videos.

Dropbox: Dropbox is a user-friendly cloud storage service that provides ample free storage space. Seniors can upload and access their digital media files from anywhere.

3. Uploading and Sharing Media

Demonstrate how to upload photos and videos to cloud storage services, making it clear that they can access these files from any internet-connected device. Seniors should also learn how to share specific files or folders with friends and family, enhancing the experience of sharing digital media.

4. Security and Privacy

Emphasize the importance of setting up secure passwords and enabling two-factor authentication (2FA) for cloud storage accounts. Seniors should be aware of the privacy settings and permissions they grant when sharing media with others.

Conclusion

Digital media, including photos and videos, has transformed the way we capture, store, and share our memories. For seniors, embracing these technologies can enhance their ability to preserve cherished moments and engage in the digital world.

By teaching seniors how to take and store photos, watch and share videos, and use cloud storage services, we empower them to navigate the digital landscape with confidence. As they become adept at capturing and sharing their experiences, they enrich their lives and strengthen connections with loved ones. Digital media opens up a world of possibilities for seniors, allowing them to relive and share their most treasured moments.

Chapter 10. Information Literacy

Introduction

In today's digital age, access to information has never been easier, yet distinguishing fact from fiction, reliable sources from questionable ones, is more challenging than ever. For seniors, information literacy is a powerful tool, enabling them to navigate the vast sea of digital information with confidence. This article explores the critical aspects of information literacy, focusing on evaluating online information for reliability, spotting fake news and misinformation, citing sources, and avoiding plagiarism.

Evaluating Online Information for Reliability

1. The Challenge of Digital Information

The internet is a treasure trove of information, but not all of it is trustworthy. The ability to evaluate the reliability of online information is crucial. Seniors must learn to distinguish credible sources from less reliable ones.

2. Source Evaluation

Teaching seniors to critically evaluate the source of information is the first step. They should assess the author's credentials, the publication's reputation, and the timeliness of the information. Encourage them to look for reputable sources, such as well-known news organizations, government websites, and academic institutions.

3. Bias and Objectivity

Seniors should understand the concept of bias in information sources. Bias can influence the way information is presented and may affect its accuracy. Encourage them to look for sources that strive for objectivity and provide multiple perspectives on a topic.

4. Fact-Checking

Seniors can use fact-checking websites and tools to verify information. Websites like Snopes, FactCheck.org, and PolitiFact provide thorough examinations of various claims, helping users confirm the accuracy of information they encounter online.

Spotting Fake News and Misinformation

1. The Proliferation of Fake News

Fake news and misinformation have become significant challenges in the digital age. Seniors need to be equipped with the skills to identify and avoid falling victim to false or misleading information.

2. Critical Thinking and Skepticism

Teaching seniors to approach online information with skepticism is key. They should question the source, the credibility of the information, and any potential bias. Encourage them to verify information by checking multiple sources before accepting it as fact.

3. Fact vs. Opinion

Help seniors distinguish between fact and opinion. Online content often includes a blend of both, and seniors should be able to differentiate objective information from subjective interpretation.

4. Identifying Red Flags

Educate seniors about common red flags that may indicate misinformation or fake news. These can include sensational or emotionally charged language, anonymous sources, and the absence of citations or references. Seniors should be cautious when encountering such content.

Citing Sources and Avoiding Plagiarism

1. Citing Sources

Seniors should understand the importance of citing sources when using information from others. This is particularly relevant if they engage in research, writing, or sharing information online. Properly citing sources gives credit to the original creators and enhances the credibility of their own work.

2. Plagiarism Awareness

Seniors must be aware of plagiarism and its consequences. Plagiarism involves using someone else's words, ideas, or work without proper attribution. Teach seniors how to paraphrase and cite sources correctly to avoid plagiarism.

3. Citation Styles

Introduce seniors to various citation styles, such as APA (American Psychological Association), MLA (Modern Language Association), and Chicago, depending on their interests and needs. Understanding the basics of these styles can help them format citations properly in their work.

4. Online Tools and Resources

Show seniors how to use online citation generators and citation management tools like Zotero or EndNote. These tools simplify the process of creating and managing citations for research projects.

Conclusion

Information literacy is a critical skill for seniors in the digital age. By empowering them with the ability to evaluate online information for reliability, spot fake news and misinformation, cite sources, and avoid plagiarism, we equip seniors to make informed decisions, participate in meaningful discussions, and engage with the digital world responsibly.

In a world where misinformation and disinformation are prevalent, seniors who possess information literacy skills become discerning consumers of information. They can confidently separate fact from fiction, identify trustworthy sources, and contribute to informed and constructive discussions both online and offline. Information literacy is not just a skill; it's a shield against the overwhelming tide of digital information, enabling seniors to navigate the digital landscape with confidence and wisdom.

Chapter 11. Online Entertainment and Hobbies

Introduction

The digital age has revolutionized the way we entertain ourselves and explore new hobbies. For seniors, embracing online entertainment and hobbies can open up a world of possibilities and enrich their lives in various ways. This article delves into the diverse facets of online entertainment and hobbies, focusing on streaming movies and TV shows and exploring online hobbies like digital art and online gaming.

Streaming Movies and TV Shows

1. The Streaming Revolution

The rise of streaming services has transformed how we consume entertainment. Seniors can enjoy their favorite movies and TV shows from the comfort of their homes, with the added convenience of choosing when and what to watch.

2. Popular Streaming Platforms

Introduce seniors to popular streaming platforms like Netflix, Amazon Prime, Hulu, and Disney+. Explain the content libraries and features of each service, helping them make informed decisions about which platforms suit their preferences.

3. How to Get Started

Teach seniors how to sign up for streaming services, create user profiles, and navigate the platforms. This includes searching for content, adding shows or movies to their watchlist, and starting or resuming playback.

4. Accessibility Features

Streaming platforms often offer accessibility features, such as closed captioning and audio descriptions, making content more inclusive. Seniors with hearing or visual impairments can learn how to enable and customize these features.

5. Online Safety

Discuss online safety with seniors, especially when they share their personal information for subscription and payment. Ensure they understand how to keep their accounts secure and avoid sharing sensitive information online.

Exploring Online Hobbies

1. Digital Art

Digital art has become increasingly popular among seniors as a creative outlet. Seniors can explore various forms of digital art, such as digital painting, illustration, and graphic design. They can use digital drawing tablets and software like Adobe Photoshop or Corel Painter to create their masterpieces.

2. Online Gaming

Online gaming offers a vast and diverse landscape of experiences. Seniors can engage in everything from casual games on smartphones to more immersive experiences on gaming consoles or computers. Multiplayer games allow them to connect with others worldwide, making online gaming a social and entertaining hobby.

3. Blogging and Writing

For seniors with a passion for writing, blogging and online publishing are excellent hobbies. Platforms like WordPress and Blogger make it easy to create and manage blogs. Seniors can share their stories, expertise, or creative writing with a global audience.

4. Online Learning and Courses

Many seniors have a desire to continue learning and expanding their knowledge. Online platforms like Coursera, edX, and Khan Academy offer free and paid courses on a wide range of subjects, allowing seniors to pursue their interests and acquire new skills.

5. Social Media and Online Communities

Seniors can use social media platforms like Facebook, Instagram, and Twitter to connect with friends and family, as well as engage in online communities dedicated to their interests and hobbies. These platforms provide a space for seniors to share their experiences and stay connected with like-minded individuals.

Conclusion

Online entertainment and hobbies offer seniors an array of opportunities to engage with the digital world in meaningful and enjoyable ways. Streaming movies and TV shows on platforms like Netflix, Amazon Prime, Hulu, and Disney+ bring an abundance of content right to their screens, giving them the freedom to choose when and what to watch.

Exploring online hobbies such as digital art, online gaming, blogging, online learning, and social media can open up new dimensions of creativity, connection, and personal growth. Seniors can nurture their artistic talents, connect with friends and family, expand their knowledge, and engage in a world of entertainment and social interaction.

Empowering seniors in the digital world means enabling them to explore their passions and interests, foster creativity, and stay connected with the world at large. These online activities can offer both entertainment and personal fulfillment, making the digital age an enriching and enjoyable phase of life for seniors.

Chapter 12. Troubleshooting and Technical Support

Introduction

In the ever-evolving digital world, technology is at the core of our daily lives. However, technical issues and challenges are bound to arise, leaving seniors feeling uncertain or even frustrated. This article aims to empower seniors with the knowledge and skills to troubleshoot common tech problems, seek help and support online, and find valuable tech resources and tutorials when needed.

Common Tech Problems and How to Fix Them

1. Slow Computer or Device

A common issue seniors face is slow device performance. They can improve this by closing unnecessary programs, uninstalling unused apps, and ensuring their device's software is up to date. Regularly restarting the device can also help speed it up.

2. Internet Connectivity Problems

Internet issues, such as a slow or disrupted connection, can be frustrating. Seniors should try restarting their router, ensuring their device is connected to the right network, and moving closer to the router to enhance the signal. If problems persist, contacting their internet service provider is a good next step.

3. Software Updates and Installation

Seniors may encounter challenges with updating or installing software. Encourage them to regularly update their operating system and apps to ensure they have the latest features and security enhancements. If they face difficulties, they should check for available support from the software's official website.

4. Lost or Forgotten Passwords

Many seniors find it challenging to manage and remember their passwords. Advise them to use password managers to securely store and auto-fill their login details. If they forget a password, they can usually reset it by clicking on the "Forgot Password" or "Reset Password" option on the login page.

5. Printer Problems

Printing issues, like paper jams or connectivity problems, can be perplexing. Seniors should consult their printer's user manual for troubleshooting guidance. Additionally, they can search for online tutorials specific to their printer model.

Seeking Help and Support Online

1. Official Product Websites

For seniors encountering technical problems with a particular device or software, the official product website is an excellent starting point. These websites typically provide user guides, FAQs, and support articles to help troubleshoot common issues.

2. Online Forums and Communities

Online tech forums and communities offer a wealth of knowledge and support. Seniors can post their technical questions or browse existing discussions to find solutions to problems. Websites like Stack Overflow and Reddit have dedicated tech support sections.

3. Tech Support Hotlines

Many tech companies offer customer support hotlines. Seniors can contact these hotlines when they encounter more complex technical issues that they cannot resolve through other means. Phone support agents can provide step-by-step guidance and solutions.

4. Social Media and Support Accounts

Some tech companies maintain social media accounts specifically for customer support. Seniors can reach out through platforms like Twitter or Facebook for assistance. Companies typically respond to inquiries on these channels.

Finding Tech Resources and Tutorials

1. Online Tech Tutorials

The internet is a treasure trove of tech tutorials and guides. Seniors can search for tutorials on platforms like YouTube or dedicated tech tutorial websites. These tutorials often provide visual step-by-step instructions for resolving common tech problems.

2. Tech Resource Websites

Websites like TechCrunch, CNET, and PCMag provide news, reviews, and resources on a wide range of tech topics. Seniors can browse these websites to stay informed about the latest tech trends and find solutions to common problems.

3. Local Community Centers and Workshops

Many local community centers offer technology workshops and classes tailored to seniors. These workshops can be a great way to learn tech skills and receive hands-on guidance.

4. Tech Podcasts and Newsletters

Seniors can explore tech podcasts and newsletters to stay updated on the latest tech developments and to access tips and tricks for navigating the digital world. Subscribing to such media can provide valuable insights.

Conclusion

Troubleshooting and technical support are invaluable skills for seniors navigating the digital world. By understanding how to resolve common tech problems, seeking help and support online, and finding tech resources and tutorials, seniors can empower themselves to address challenges and harness the potential of technology in their daily lives.

Empowering seniors in the digital world goes beyond teaching them how to use devices; it also involves arming them with the skills to tackle technical obstacles independently. By fostering a problem-solving mindset and providing access to a variety of resources, we ensure that seniors can confidently navigate the ever-evolving digital landscape. In doing so, they can participate in the digital age with enthusiasm and autonomy.

Chapter 13. Staying Up-to-Date

Introduction

In the fast-paced world of technology, staying up-to-date is essential to make the most of digital tools and innovations. For seniors, embracing the digital world and harnessing its benefits can be an empowering experience. This article explores the critical aspects of staying up-to-date, focusing on keeping software and devices updated, and following technology news and trends.

Keeping Software and Devices Updated

1. The Importance of Software Updates

Software updates are vital for maintaining the performance, security, and functionality of digital devices. Keeping devices and software up-to-date is an essential practice for seniors to ensure a smooth and secure digital experience.

2. Operating System Updates

Operating system updates, such as Windows, macOS, and Android, often include bug fixes, performance enhancements, and security patches. Seniors should regularly check for and install these updates to ensure their devices are running optimally.

3. App and Software Updates

Apps and software also require regular updates. Seniors should enable automatic updates whenever possible to ensure they have the latest features and security improvements. Encourage them to explore the app settings and configure automatic updates for their favorite applications.

4. Hardware Firmware Updates

In addition to software updates, some hardware devices, like routers and smart home gadgets, may require firmware updates. Seniors should check the manufacturer's website or the device's settings for available updates and follow the instructions to install them.

5. Benefits of Regular Updates

Highlight the benefits of keeping software and devices up-to-date, such as improved performance, enhanced security against malware and cyber threats, and access to new features that can make their digital experiences more enjoyable and efficient.

Following Technology News and Trends

1. The Rapid Evolution of Technology

The digital world evolves rapidly, with new technologies and trends emerging constantly. Seniors can empower themselves by staying informed about these changes and understanding how they can impact their digital experiences.

2. Technology News Sources

Introduce seniors to reliable technology news sources, such as websites, magazines, podcasts, and YouTube channels. Some trusted tech news outlets include CNET, TechCrunch, The Verge, and Wired. Seniors can explore these sources to learn about the latest gadgets, software updates, and tech innovations.

3. Subscribing to Newsletters

Encourage seniors to subscribe to newsletters that provide regular updates on technology trends and innovations. These newsletters often offer curated content, making it easier for seniors to stay informed without overwhelming them with excessive information.

4. Tech Blogs and Forums

Blogs and forums are excellent platforms for discussing tech topics and seeking advice. Seniors can follow tech blogs or participate in online forums to engage with like-minded individuals, ask questions, and share their experiences.

5. Attending Tech Workshops and Webinars

Many organizations offer tech workshops and webinars, both in-person and online. These events provide seniors with opportunities to learn about emerging technologies and trends, as well as ask questions and receive guidance from experts.

Conclusion

Staying up-to-date in the digital world is an essential component of seniors' empowerment. By keeping software and devices updated, seniors can ensure that their digital tools run smoothly and securely, enhancing their overall digital experience.

Additionally, following technology news and trends enables seniors to remain informed about the latest innovations, which can enhance their digital literacy and encourage them to explore new possibilities. Understanding emerging technologies allows seniors to adapt to the changing digital landscape with confidence and enthusiasm.

Empowering seniors in the digital world means arming them with the knowledge and skills to make the most of digital tools and innovations. By staying up-to-date, they can navigate the ever-evolving digital landscape with grace, maintaining their independence and taking full advantage of the benefits technology has to offer.

Chapter 14. Digital Etiquette and Ethics

Introduction

The digital world is a vast and diverse landscape, but one constant remains: the importance of etiquette and ethics. For seniors, understanding digital etiquette, also known as netiquette, and adhering to ethical principles is essential to navigate the digital realm with respect and responsibility. This article explores the critical aspects of digital etiquette and ethics, focusing on online etiquette, respecting copyright and intellectual property, and the importance of ethical online behavior.

Online Etiquette and Netiquette

1. The Basics of Online Etiquette

Digital etiquette, commonly referred to as netiquette, encompasses a set of guidelines for polite and respectful behavior in the digital world. These principles are the foundation of positive online interactions.

2. Communication Respect

Seniors should be mindful of their communication in digital spaces. This includes using respectful language, refraining from offensive or hurtful comments, and avoiding online arguments or conflicts. Encourage seniors to treat others online as they would in face-to-face conversations.

3. Privacy and Security

Emphasize the importance of respecting privacy and security. Seniors should be cautious about sharing personal information, both their own and that of others. Encourage them to use strong, unique passwords, and to recognize phishing attempts and scams.

4. Online Discussions and Forums

Participating in online discussions and forums can be rewarding, but it's important to maintain respect and civility. Seniors should express their opinions respectfully, refrain from spamming, and avoid overusing capital letters (considered online shouting).

5. Understanding Online Norms

Explain to seniors that online spaces often have their own norms and conventions. Encourage them to familiarize themselves with the specific rules and expectations of the online communities they join.

Respecting Copyright and Intellectual Property

1. The Importance of Copyright

Copyright laws protect the creative works of authors, artists, and content creators. Seniors should be aware that using someone else's work without proper permission or attribution is a violation of copyright.

2. Avoiding Plagiarism

Seniors should understand the concept of plagiarism. Encourage them to always give credit to the original creators when using their content, whether it's text, images, music, or videos. Show seniors how to properly cite sources and provide attribution.

3. Public Domain and Creative Commons

Teach seniors about public domain works and Creative Commons licenses. Public domain works are not protected by copyright and can be used freely. Creative Commons licenses allow creators to specify how others can use their work, such as requiring attribution or allowing derivative works.

4. Fair Use

Explain the concept of fair use, which allows limited use of copyrighted material without permission for purposes like commentary, criticism, or education. Seniors should be aware of the factors that determine fair use and understand its limitations.

5. Using Images and Content

Seniors often use images and content for personal projects or sharing online. Teach them how to find and use content with proper licensing and attribution. Websites like Pixabay, Unsplash, and Wikimedia Commons offer a wealth of free and openly licensed images.

Conclusion

Digital etiquette and ethics are fundamental in the digital age, guiding seniors to navigate the online world with respect, responsibility, and integrity. Understanding online etiquette, or netiquette, is crucial to fostering positive and meaningful digital interactions. It ensures that seniors communicate respectfully, protect their privacy, and participate in online communities with civility.

Respecting copyright and intellectual property is equally essential. Seniors should understand that using someone else's work without permission or proper attribution is a violation of copyright and unethical. By practicing good digital etiquette and respecting copyright, seniors can contribute to a more constructive and harmonious digital environment.

Empowering seniors in the digital world goes beyond technical skills; it also encompasses ethical and respectful behavior. By embracing digital etiquette and respecting copyright, seniors can not only thrive in the digital landscape but also set an example of responsible and considerate online conduct for generations to come.

Chapter 15. Connecting with Family and Friends

Introduction

In the digital age, staying connected with family and friends has never been easier, and for seniors, this connectivity can be truly empowering. This article explores the various ways seniors can connect with their loved ones in the digital world. It focuses on using social media to stay in touch and highlights the possibilities of online family reunions and gatherings.

Using Social Media for Staying in Touch

1. The Power of Social Media

Social media platforms have revolutionized the way people connect and communicate. For seniors, these platforms offer a convenient way to stay in touch with family and friends, even when they're separated by great distances.

2. Choosing the Right Platform

There are various social media platforms available, each with its unique features and audience. Encourage seniors to choose a platform that aligns with their preferences and that most of their loved ones are using. Common choices include Facebook, Instagram, Twitter, and LinkedIn.

3. Setting Up a Profile

Help seniors create and set up their social media profiles. Guide them through the process of adding profile pictures, writing a bio, and configuring privacy settings to control who can see their posts and interact with them.

4. Connecting with Family and Friends

Seniors can search for and connect with family and friends using their email addresses or usernames. They should also explore the option to import contacts from their email address book to find connections easily.

5. Sharing Updates and Photos

Once connected, seniors can share updates, photos, and videos with their loved ones. Encourage them to post about their daily experiences, celebrations, or special moments. This helps family and friends feel more connected to their lives.

Online Family Reunions and Gatherings

1. The Concept of Virtual Gatherings

Virtual gatherings are a fantastic way to bring the family together, even when physical distances make traditional reunions challenging. These gatherings can include family reunions, birthday parties, holidays, or any special occasion.

2. Selecting a Platform for Virtual Gatherings

Platforms like Zoom, Skype, and Google Meet are ideal for hosting virtual family gatherings. Seniors can install these applications on their devices and share invitations with family members.

3. Scheduling and Planning

Seniors can take an active role in scheduling and planning virtual gatherings. They can coordinate with family members to select a date and time that works for everyone and set up the virtual meeting.

4. Participating in Virtual Gatherings

During the virtual gathering, seniors can engage in conversations, share stories, and participate in games or activities, just like they would during in-person gatherings. These gatherings provide a sense of togetherness, even when family members are miles apart.

5. Recording Memories

Many virtual meeting platforms allow users to record sessions. Seniors can capture these moments to revisit and relive family gatherings. This can be particularly meaningful when family members are spread across different parts of the world.

Conclusion

In the digital age, seniors have the opportunity to bridge physical distances and stay closely connected with their family and friends. By using social media for staying in touch and participating in online family reunions and gatherings, seniors can experience the warmth of human relationships and create lasting memories.

Empowering seniors in the digital world is not just about mastering technology; it's about leveraging it to enhance the quality of their lives. Through the power of digital connectivity, seniors can maintain their emotional bonds with family and friends, no matter where they are in the world. Digital tools enable seniors to experience the joy of sharing life's moments and celebrating together, enriching their lives in meaningful ways.

Chapter 16. Building Confidence and Overcoming Fear

Introduction

The digital world is a dynamic and ever-evolving landscape, offering a wealth of opportunities and connections. However, for seniors, embracing this new world can be intimidating, and many are plagued by fears and uncertainties. In this article, we explore the vital aspect of building confidence and overcoming fear in the digital realm. We will address common fears and concerns about technology and provide guidance on building self-assurance through practice and learning.

Addressing Common Fears and Concerns About Technology

1. The Fear of the Unknown

One of the most common fears among seniors is the fear of the unknown. The rapidly evolving technology landscape can be daunting, making many seniors hesitant to explore it.

2. Fear of Making Mistakes

Seniors often worry about making mistakes, fearing that they might break something or make errors that are irreversible. The fear of technology mishaps can be paralyzing.

3. Privacy and Security Concerns

Privacy and security are significant concerns for seniors. They may worry about identity theft, scams, or unintentionally sharing personal information online.

4. Feeling Left Behind

The feeling of being left behind by younger generations who seem naturally tech-savvy can lead to self-doubt and a sense of isolation.

5. Complex Terminology

Technology is rife with complex jargon and terminology that can be intimidating. Seniors may fear that they won't understand or keep up with the ever-evolving tech language.

Building Self-Assurance Through Practice and Learning

1. Taking Small Steps

The journey to digital confidence starts with taking small, manageable steps. Seniors should not feel pressured to master everything at once. Encourage them to begin with basic tasks like sending an email, searching the internet, or using a smartphone camera.

2. Seeking Support and Guidance

Seniors should seek support from friends, family, or local resources. Many communities offer tech classes specifically designed for seniors. A supportive environment where they can ask questions and learn at their own pace can be invaluable.

3. Online Resources and Tutorials

The internet is a vast source of information and tutorials. Seniors can explore platforms like YouTube, Khan Academy, or educational websites that offer easy-to-follow lessons on various digital topics.

4. Practicing Patience and Persistence

Building digital confidence requires patience and persistence. Seniors should understand that they may encounter challenges and setbacks along the way. These moments are part of the learning process, not failures.

5. Overcoming Fear of Mistakes

Seniors should be encouraged to embrace the possibility of making mistakes as a valuable learning experience. They should remember that even experienced tech users make mistakes, and errors are a natural part of the learning journey.

Building Confidence Over Time

1. Understanding Privacy and Security

Seniors can build confidence by educating themselves about online privacy and security. They should learn about the importance of strong, unique passwords and be cautious about sharing personal information online.

2. Staying Updated

Encourage seniors to stay updated with technology news and trends. By keeping abreast of the latest developments, they can gradually overcome the fear of being left behind.

3. Empowering Self-Expression

Technology can be a tool for self-expression and creativity. Seniors should explore opportunities to express themselves through digital media, whether it's writing, photography, or even starting a blog or social media account.

4. Connecting with Family and Friends

Seniors can find motivation and support by using technology to connect with family and friends. Video calls, email, and social media provide a means to stay connected and share experiences.

Conclusion

Building confidence and overcoming fear in the digital world is a journey, not a destination. By addressing common fears and concerns about technology, seniors can recognize and acknowledge their worries. It is essential to encourage seniors to take small, manageable steps and seek guidance and support from resources and communities designed to help them.

Digital confidence is built over time through learning and practice. Seniors should remember that making mistakes is a natural part of the learning process and that everyone, regardless of age, encounters challenges when embracing technology. In the digital world, seniors can connect with others, express themselves, and stay informed about the latest developments, gradually overcoming the fear of the unknown.

Empowering seniors in the digital world involves nurturing their self-assurance and guiding them to navigate the digital landscape with confidence and curiosity. By addressing fears, seeking support, and embracing the learning journey, seniors can harness the benefits of technology, enrich their lives, and remain engaged in the ever-evolving digital world.

Chapter 17. Resources for Ongoing Learning

Introduction

Learning is a lifelong journey, and in today's digital age, seniors have an unprecedented opportunity to expand their knowledge and skills. This article delves into the essential resources for ongoing learning that empower seniors in the digital world. It will explore online courses and tutorials, local community resources and classes, and how technology can help seniors overcome challenges and achieve their learning goals.

Online Courses and Tutorials

1. The Expansive World of Online Learning

The internet offers a vast array of online courses and tutorials covering diverse subjects, from art and history to technology and science. Seniors can explore these resources to fuel their passion for learning and gain new skills.

2. Popular Online Learning Platforms

There are several reputable online learning platforms that offer a wide range of courses. Seniors can explore options like Coursera, edX, Udemy, and Khan Academy, each with its unique course catalog and teaching style.

3. Choosing the Right Course

Selecting the right course is essential. Seniors should consider their interests and goals, ensuring they choose a course that resonates with their aspirations. They can explore course descriptions, reviews, and previews to make informed decisions.

4. The Flexibility of Online Learning

One of the advantages of online learning is its flexibility. Seniors can choose when and where they want to study, allowing them to fit learning into their daily routines.

5. Tech Skills for Online Learning

Learning online often requires basic tech skills. Seniors should become familiar with online navigation, video conferencing, and document sharing. They can ask for help from friends or family members or take basic tech classes to become more comfortable with these tools.

Local Community Resources and Classes

1. Community Centers and Senior Programs

Many local communities offer resources and classes for seniors. Community centers and senior programs provide a supportive and welcoming environment where seniors can connect with peers and engage in various learning activities.

2. Exploring Local Courses

Seniors should explore the courses offered in their community. This might include art classes, cooking workshops, gardening clubs, or even local history lectures. Participating in these courses can provide an enriching and social learning experience.

3. Library Resources

Public libraries are a treasure trove of learning resources. Seniors can visit their local library to access books, audiobooks, and digital resources. Many libraries offer e-books and digital audiobooks, making it easy to access a wide range of educational content.

4. Connecting with Local Instructors

Local instructors and experts can provide seniors with hands-on guidance and knowledge. Seniors should reach out to local artists, craftsmen, or hobbyists for mentoring or collaboration on learning projects.

5. Joining Senior Clubs and Organizations

Many senior clubs and organizations host activities and events that promote learning and social interaction. Seniors can consider joining clubs related to their interests, whether it's a book club, a gardening group, or a history society.

Overcoming Challenges and Achieving Goals Through Technology

1. Setting Clear Learning Goals

To make the most of the available resources, seniors should set clear learning goals. They should outline what they want to achieve, whether it's acquiring a new skill, exploring a new hobby, or gaining in-depth knowledge of a particular subject.

2. Connecting with a Learning Community

Seniors can benefit from joining online forums or social media groups related to their interests. Engaging with a learning community can provide a support system, foster discussions, and create opportunities for collaboration.

3. Seeking Help and Support

Seniors should never hesitate to seek help and support when needed. Whether they encounter technical challenges, need clarification on a course topic, or want guidance from a local instructor, they should reach out to experts and peers.

4. Technology as an Accessibility Tool

For seniors with physical limitations or mobility challenges, technology can serve as an accessibility tool. Voice recognition software, screen readers, and adaptive devices can help make digital content and resources more accessible.

5. Embracing Lifelong Learning

Lifelong learning is a mindset. Seniors should embrace the idea that learning is a continuous and fulfilling part of life. By staying curious, exploring new interests, and engaging with diverse learning resources, they can empower themselves with knowledge and personal growth.

Conclusion

Resources for ongoing learning are a cornerstone of empowerment for seniors in the digital world. Whether through online courses and tutorials, local community resources and classes, or the supportive embrace of technology, seniors can continue to broaden their horizons, discover new interests, and achieve personal and intellectual goals.

Empowering seniors in the digital age means nurturing their passion for learning and providing them with the tools and resources they need to keep their minds active and engaged. The journey of learning is a lifelong adventure, and with the right resources and the support of their communities, seniors can continue to thrive in their pursuit of knowledge and personal growth.

Chapter 18. Glossary of Digital Terms

This glossary provides definitions and explanations for common digital terms and concepts discussed throughout the book, "Empowering Seniors in the Digital World". As seniors embark on their digital literacy journey, understanding these terms will help them navigate the digital landscape with confidence and ease.

Accessibility: Accessibility in the digital context refers to the design and implementation of digital content and technology to ensure that individuals with disabilities can access and use them effectively.

Adaptive Devices: Adaptive devices are specialized tools or hardware designed to assist individuals with physical or sensory disabilities in using digital devices and technology.

Cloud Storage: Cloud storage is a service that allows users to store and access their data, such as files and photos, on remote servers via the internet. It provides a convenient way to back up and access data from multiple devices.

Community Resources: Community resources refer to local organizations, centers, and programs that offer support, services, and activities to individuals within a specific geographical area.

Copyright: Copyright is a legal protection that grants creators exclusive rights to their original works, such as writings, art, and music. It prevents others from using, copying, or distributing the work without permission.

Digital Art: Digital art is a form of artistic expression that uses digital technology, such as computers, tablets, and graphics software, to create visual artworks, illustrations, and designs.

Digital Etiquette: Digital etiquette, also known as netiquette, involves adhering to polite and respectful behavior when interacting with others in online and digital environments.

Digital Literacy: Digital literacy refers to the ability to use digital devices, software, and the internet to access, create, and share information. It encompasses skills related to technology usage, online safety, and information literacy.

Digital Divide: The digital divide refers to the gap between those who have access to digital technology and the internet and those who do not. It can result in disparities in access to information, education, and opportunities.

E-commerce: E-commerce, short for electronic commerce, is the buying and selling of goods and services over the internet. It involves online shopping, online payments, and online marketplaces.

Email: Email, short for electronic mail, is a method of sending and receiving messages electronically over the internet. It is a common form of online communication.

Email Scams: Email scams are fraudulent or deceptive messages sent through email with the intent of tricking recipients into taking harmful actions, such as revealing personal information or sending money.

Fake News: Fake news refers to intentionally false or misleading information presented as legitimate news. It is designed to deceive readers and spread misinformation.

Information Literacy: Information literacy is the ability to evaluate, analyze, and use information from various sources critically. It involves distinguishing reliable information from unreliable or biased sources.

Intellectual Growth: Intellectual growth refers to the development of one's mental abilities, knowledge, and critical thinking skills through learning and educational experiences.

Intellectual Property: Intellectual property refers to creations of the mind, including inventions, literary and artistic works, and symbols. It is protected by copyright, patents, and trademarks.

Learning Community: A learning community is a group of individuals who come together to share knowledge, resources, and experiences related to a common interest or field of study.

Lifelong Adventure: Lifelong adventure reflects the idea that learning is an exciting and continuous journey that offers opportunities for exploration, discovery, and personal fulfillment.

Lifelong Learning: Lifelong learning is the continuous pursuit of knowledge, skills, and personal development throughout one's life. It involves a commitment to ongoing education and self-improvement.

Online Banking: Online banking enables users to manage their financial accounts, check balances, transfer funds, pay bills, and conduct other banking activities through secure internet banking platforms.

Online Courses: Online courses are educational programs offered on the internet, allowing students to learn and acquire knowledge in various subjects through online lessons, assignments, and assessments.

Online Forums: Online forums, also known as discussion boards or message boards, are web-based platforms where users can engage in discussions, ask questions, and share information on various topics.

Online Gaming: Online gaming involves playing video games or computer games over the internet with other players, either collaboratively or competitively, in a virtual environment.

Online Scams: Online scams are fraudulent schemes or activities conducted on the internet with the goal of deceiving users and often extracting money or personal information.

Online Shopping: Online shopping refers to the process of purchasing products or services through e-commerce websites and apps. It allows users to browse, select, and make secure transactions online.

Password: A password is a secret combination of characters used to authenticate and access online accounts. It serves as a security measure to protect personal information.

Phishing: Phishing is a form of cyberattack in which attackers impersonate legitimate entities to trick individuals into revealing sensitive information, such as usernames, passwords, or credit card details.

Plagiarism: Plagiarism is the act of using someone else's work, ideas, or words without proper attribution or permission. It is considered unethical and can have academic or legal consequences.

Screen Reader: A screen reader is assistive technology that reads aloud the content displayed on a computer or mobile device screen. It is designed to help individuals with visual impairments access digital content.

Search Engine: A search engine is a web-based tool that allows users to search for information on the internet. Google, Bing, and Yahoo are examples of search engines.

Social Media: Social media platforms are websites and apps that allow users to create, share, and interact with content and other users. Examples include Facebook, Twitter, and Instagram.

Streaming: Streaming is the process of delivering digital media content, such as music, movies, or TV shows, over the internet in real-time. Users can watch or listen to the content without downloading it.

Tech Problems: Tech problems refer to issues or challenges that individuals encounter when using digital devices or software. They can range from minor glitches to more complex technical issues.

Tech Resources: Tech resources are materials, websites, and tools that provide information, guidance, and solutions for digital and technology-related topics and challenges.

URL (Uniform Resource Locator): A URL is a web address that specifies the location of a web resource on the internet. It typically includes the protocol (e.g., "http" or "https"), domain name (e.g., "www.example.com"), and specific path or page.

Video Call: A video call is a real-time communication method that allows individuals to see and hear each other using video and audio over the internet. Platforms like Skype and Zoom facilitate video calls.

Voice Recognition Software: Voice recognition software, also known as speech recognition software, allows users to control a computer or device using spoken commands. It converts spoken words into text or actions.

Web Browser: A web browser is a software application used to access and view websites on the internet. Popular web browsers include Google Chrome, Mozilla Firefox, and Microsoft Edge.

Web Resources: Web resources refer to online materials, websites, and platforms that provide information, educational content, and digital services.

"Empowering Seniors in the Digital World" is a comprehensive guide designed to bridge the generation gap in technology, enabling seniors to confidently navigate the digital landscape. This book provides a step-by-step journey, starting with the importance of digital literacy and addressing the digital divide. It covers essential topics like selecting the right devices, mastering internet skills, and safe email communication.

Readers will also learn to harness the power of social media, prioritize online safety, explore e-commerce and digital media, and gain valuable information literacy skills. Additionally, it empowers seniors to connect with family and friends and foster their self-assurance. With practical advice, troubleshooting tips, and a handy glossary of digital terms, this book is a trusted companion for seniors looking to embrace the digital age with confidence and ease.

ABOUT THE AUTHOR

Mr. C. P. Kumar is a retired Scientist 'G' from National Institute of Hydrology, Roorkee, Uttarakhand, India. He is also a Reiki Healer and Chakra Balancing practitioner (with pendulum dowsing) and offers Emotional Freedom Technique (EFT) to help individuals with emotional issues. Mr. Kumar has authored many books on technical, spiritual, and social topics.

For further details, you may visit his webpage
https://www.angelfire.com/nh/cpkumar/virgo.html

www.ingramcontent.com/pod-product-compliance
Lightning Source LLC
Chambersburg PA
CBHW071302050326
40690CB00011B/2505